LOVE

IS AN

ATTITUDE

WALTER RINDER

LOVE IS AN ATTITUDE

WALTER RINDER

CELESTIAL ARTS
Millbrae, California

First printing: December 1970
                17 18 − 82 81 80 79 78

ISBN: 0-912310-03-0

Library of Congress Catalog Card Number 74-147246

Printed in the United States of America

Preface

"Words," says Rinder, "are limiting. Better to weave with the simple ones, close to the senses." Herein lies a solution to the confrontation between traditional language and expanding Consciousness ... with poetry and photography sent to satisfy our souls, smooth our jagged edges, and quench a generation's thirst for simplicity, community, and love. Rinder's is a natural trip, relying on the only useful language known to man: the distillation of a universal plea for peace between men, and within them. His camera and pen reinforce the renaissance of our senses, and he fully believes that "the greatest thing a poet or a teacher can do for people is to discover them to themselves." So go with this poet and find—you!

DEDICATION

This book I dedicate to all the people who have openly given me so very much love and understanding, especially my mother and father.

Those years when I was very young and searching for my identity were filled with loneliness and the struggle to find beauty when beauty was so often lost in the maze of our impersonal society. As I traveled the countryside, from town to town, love would find me and enter, but only if the door of my heart was open to it. Now I have torn down that door and in its place have built an archway that is always opened to love.

May this creative endeavor bring the sensitivity of love closer to your heart, opening you up to yourself.

LOVE IS AN ATTITUDE

Today is a beautiful day!
The rays of light filtered
through the sentinels of
trees this morning.
I sat by the creek and
contemplated.
I missed classes, but
somehow it didn't matter.
The serenity and beauty
of my feelings and
surroundings completely
captivated me . . .

I thought of you.
I discovered you tucked
away in the shadows of the
trees. Then rediscovered
you on the smiles of the
flowers as the sun
penetrated the petals . . .
in the rhythm of the leaves
falling upon the stream . . .
in the freedom of the
robin as he flew searching
as you do.

I'm very happy to have
found you again.
Now, you will never leave
me, for I will always find
you in the beauty of life.

This was a special place when I clawed
my way to freedom, away from the city
    Meditating upon the rocks
    melting into the icy water
    inhaling the salt air—
my mind commenced to heal
I wrote . . . I thought . . . I swam . . .
I slept
One day a stranger entered my domain
and my solitude was transformed
into love

Will we see the day when, again, nature becomes the teacher of man?

Music echoed across . . . valleys and mountains and cities where he called home, even for but a short while. The songs he sang were as the **minstrels,** folk songs and short episodes of his wonderings.

We used to listen to his tales in front of the old red house, when he once came our way, and we drifted into his world with him. We never knew where he came from or where he was going. He made our lives a little fuller and set us to thinking.

escape the sorrow of yesterday's
love unheeded,
tomorrow's love unfulfilled . . .
Love Now!

Because you are afraid to love
I am alone.

Yesterday's hurt
Is today's understanding
Rewoven into tomorrow's love.

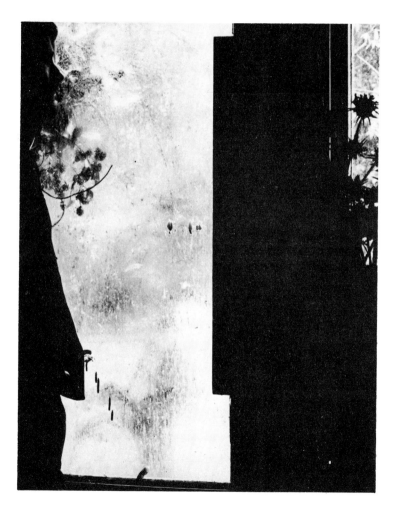

Love comes as birth does . . .
knowing its own time.

Nothing is more wondrous than a human being when he begins to discover himself.

The soul can rise from the earth
into the sky, like a bird
aware of its freedom,
not feeling the barriers of man
but the beauty of love
which is eternal.

To MY BELOVED

I love you freely without restrictions
I love your understanding without doubt
I love you honestly without deceit
I love you creatively without conditioning
I love you now without reservation
I love you physically without pretending
I love your soul without wishing
I love your being without wanting
I love you.

Don't look away from the world
Give yourself to it.

Which has more substance, the
thought of love or
an act of love?

All that we love, deeply
becomes a part of us.

The natural know only innocence.

We are all mirrors unto one another.
Look into me and you will find something of yourself as I will of you.

 DAY HAS VANISHED. The sun has dropped like a penny into the pocket of the night. The sounds of the day-light hours have given way to quiet solitude. Fog is creeping in, engulfing the cypress trees, erasing my view of the ocean, hiding the moon that lights my wondering along the shore.

Where are you! Where did you go! Let me feel your touch. Don't let this moment slip away from us. Listen, hear, the sea gull. He's searching too. Please take my hand; it's extended for you.

See the footprints in the sand, traveling from shore to shore. The tide will wash away those footprints but tomorrow there will be new ones. There always are. Take my hand. We've a long way to go. A lifetime.

How small
   a grain of sand
a whisp of hair
   and man!
How large
   a grain of time
a whisp of giving
   and love.

I was alone, walking in the park
You were sitting by a tree.
Our eyes met.
You smiled.

Nature the teacher, man the student.

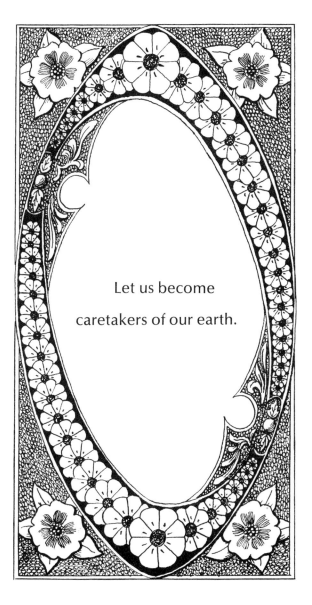

Let us become

caretakers of our earth.

Love and nature,
a fulfillment of one's self.

Into my mouth place a crust of bread
So as hunger may not gnaw into my soul
Clothe my body with loving care
Mend my heart from a broken lance
Give me courage with a fervent glance
Bring me contentment in softened tones
Guide my knowledge with truth serene
To continue my life in meaningful purpose
Show me the way through the human maze
Guide my confusion into simpler days.

The tide washes in . . .
I walk with thoughts of the dreamer's wine
and a thousand nights pass
mirrored by the sea.

I fear no love—
For my heart is open,
My mind sincere,
And my actions honorable.

Have you ever listened to the snowfall?

SPECTRUM OF LOVE

"I love you."

There is a much greater motivation than simply my spoken words.

For me to love, is to commit myself, freely and without reservation. I am sincerely interested in your happiness and well being. Whatever your needs are, I will try to fulfill them and will bend in my values depending on the importance of your need. If you are lonely and need me, I will be there. If in that loneliness you need to talk, I will listen. If you need to listen, I will talk. If you need the strength of human touch, I will touch you. If you need to be held, I will hold you. I will lie naked in body with you if that be your need. If you need fulfillment of the flesh, I will give you that also, but only through my love.

I will try to be constant with you so that you will understand the core of my personality and from that understanding you can gain strength and security that I am acting as me. I may falter with my moods. I may project, at times, a strangeness that is alien to you which may bewilder or frighten you. There will be times when you question my motives. But because people are never constant and are as changeable as the seasons, I will try to build up within you a faith in my fundamental attitude and show you that my inconsistency is only for the moment and not a lasting part of me. I will show you love now. Each and every day, for each day is a lifetime. Every day we live, we learn more how to love. I will not defer my love nor neglect it, for if I wait until tomorrow, tomorrow never comes. It is like a cloud in the sky, passing by. They always do you know!

If I give you kindness and understanding, then I will receive your faith. If I give hate and dishonesty, I will receive your distrust. If I give you fear and am afraid, you will become afraid and fear me. I will give to you what I need to receive.

The degree of love I give is determined by my own capability. My capability is determined by the environment of my past existence and my understanding of love, truth and God. My understanding is determined by my parents, friends, places I have lived and been. Each experience is fed into my mind from living.

I will give you as much love as I can. If you will show me how to give more, then I will give more. I can only give as much as you need to receive or allow me to give. If you receive all I can give, then my love is endless and fulfilled. If you receive a portion (part) of my love, then I will give others the balance I am capable of giving. I must give all that I have, being what I am.

Love is universal. Love is the movement of life. I have loved a boy, a girl, my parents, art, nature. All things in life I find beautiful. No human being or society has the right to condemn any kind of love I feel or my way of expressing it, if I am sincere; sincerity being the honest realization of myself without hurt or pain for my life or any life my life touches.

I want to become a truly loving spirit. Let my words, if I must speak, become a restoration of your soul. But when speech is silent, does a man project the great depth of his sensitivity. When I touch you, or kiss you, or hold you, I am saying a thousand words.

Do not reject what you do not understand; for with understanding there may be acceptance

Take time with each other.
Let the seed of love grow and
flourish with the seasons;
Spring's awareness
Summer's warmth
Autumn's understanding
Winter's serenity

To be of few words and to be of many actions is to follow the path of nature.

A storm does not drop all its rain in one place, nor does a river have one tributary, or is there just one wave in the ocean, or does the sun always shine. Rather, a continued variation and repetition of acts gives the harmony and balance to nature. This is what we should strive for: Love in all forms and all kinds becomes the harmony of man.

Help me to unite myself with life
through your love.

Love cannot be begged, bought,
borrowed or stolen.
It can only be given away.

The greatest path toward truth is experiencing life by crawling in its dirt and being lifted by the wings of its beauty.

HANDS

Our hands are extensions of our heart, through their movements people know what we are, who we are, and how we feel.

Take hold of someone's hand. You can feel the beating of their heart, the very substance of their life.

The hand has as many expressions as the face and if you don't see any reactions from the face watch their hands . . . covering their face in desperation, reaching out for warmth, caressing your body with love, clawing to push death away, tension in holding something, their motion in creating, their movements in happiness, stillness in idleness or loneliness.

The shape of the hands follows the structure of the body, heavy, thin, muscular, fragile, strong, smooth, rough.

Our mind is the energy. Our hands the projection of that energy.

Take someone's hand and you will have, in that moment, begun the awareness of yourself. That moment has the seed of the creation of love, every time it is done.

Use your hands in the pursuit of beauty, adding and building of life.

The hands are so very sensitive to the elements of nature. Feel the bark of a tree. Put your hands in the snow or a cold stream. Run your fingers across the sand. Put your hands near a fire. Hold your hands up to the rain or the sun or the wind, all different feelings. Touch the coat of a dog or the skin of a snake.

As the years pass your hands gain knowledge as does your mind, and grow older as does your body.

Your hands carry episodes of your life: scarred, stained, calloused, scratched.

Let your hands become the joining together of you and another human being, the extension of your heart, the merging of two rivers, the grafting of two branches, the birth of new life.

Your hands are you.

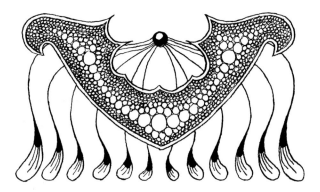

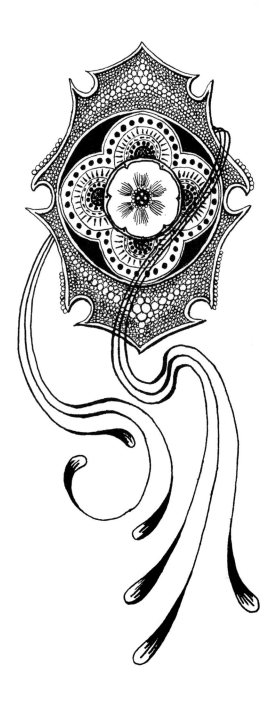

Love is an attitude . . .
   in constant motion as the sea.

Remember by finding things
within yourself
only then will you be able to
share them with others.

The harmony and balance
of nature is one of
the greatest lessons to man.

LAST NIGHT IT RAINED. I saw your face through the clouded window pane. It seemed you were crying but it was only the rain falling down the window. I heard your laughter but it was only the thunder repeating itself. I thought I heard you talking to me but it was only the branches rubbing against the glass.

It's morning now. The rain has stopped.

We do not need words.
Our eyes speak
our touch reveals.
Each new day we discover new beauty
in silence, of each other.

Live for today but
remember yesterday
and think of tomorrow.

We should receive love
with as much understanding
as we give love.

FIVE FACES IN A ROOM

Five faces in a room
    each reflecting a soul
        five faces in a room
            each wanting to be whole.

Five faces in a room
    staring into space
        five faces in a room
            mustn't lose the race.

Five faces in a room
    their longing unfulfilled
        five faces in a room
            Their love is quietly stilled.

Five faces in a room
    wanting to relate
        five faces in a room
            trying to create.

Five faces in a room
    talking, laughing, reading
        five faces in a room
            everyone is leaving.

We see with our eyes, but not our **mind**
We touch with our hands, but not our **heart**
We laugh with our lips, but not our **soul**
We express affection with our body
                              but not our **love**
We lie in bed naked together but not **united**

On this "Speck of Earth," together we can make love, only if we transform ourselves into the trees and vegetation that surround us, so that we are not seen by human beings. For someone, somewhere will say of us, "our love is wrong."

They don't understand!

A thousand years is but a
grain of sand in time . . . but love
is a thousand grains of sand in
one human lifetime.

PEOPLE OF EARTH

How accelerated your lives have become ... not begun! ... you ... people of the earth, integrated into ant hills you call cities. Caught in the whirlpool of your society, bringing you deeper and deeper into your concrete jungle of asphalt, cement mountains covering the sun, stagnant air as your sky, status symbols of synthetics, overcrowding, waiting in lines, hurrying to where! Freeways, byways, traffic jams, headaches, tension, alcohol, drugs, insecurity, not caring, being afraid ... and whatever happened to love?

You surround yourselves with progress ... Like living on an island without a boat.

Are you really happy? Does progress bring you a fulfillment within your soul?

You are a part of nature, you come from the earth, from the seed of life. You are alienated when you depart from the original beauty of your environment. You possess a soul. So does nature ... And when you are together you speak deep thoughts, not in words, but in feelings ...

REMEMBER ... when the warm sun followed you as you ran freely along the ocean's shores; the sand was warm when your feet pressed into its softness; the wind was pure as it lifted your hair dancing to the rhythm of your movements; and how the salt water tingled your body as it dried crisp on your golden skin . . . THE SUN WAS ALIVE.

REMEMBER . . . when you heard the laughter of the waves as they splashed and played with the rocks; the harmonious colors of the ocean as she dressed for the new day; and the gentle kiss of the water as it died in the arms of the shore to be reborn again far out at sea . . . THE OCEAN WAS ALIVE.

REMEMBER . . . the little tide pool you found hidden among the rocks; so serene, so clean, so transparent, and within its depths lay pieces of colored shells, a starfish or two; beautiful emerald green sea urchins; delicate pink anemones; and tiny fish darting to and fro; a world within a world . . . THE POOL WAS ALIVE.

As you began departing from nature, nature said of you: "I know man is leaving me, but I welcome him to return when he wishes, for I love him and want him to always be a part of me, sharing our hidden secrets." You seldom went back to nature and all is almost forgotten . . . PROGRESS HAS ENSLAVED YOU . . . PROGRESS HAS BECOME A TYRANT AND YOU HIS SLAVE.
. . . FREE YOURSELVES . . . people of earth.

Cut the shackles that bind you. Open the door of your mind, TO AWARENESS—as you look into the sky, into the ocean, upon the valleys and the mountains, and you will shed tears of happiness as you feel the rain run down your cheeks, as you feel the snowflakes melt upon your hands, as you feel the sun give warmth to your body and as you feel the wind embrace you.
FOR IN NATURE WITH MAN THERE IS LOVE...
SHARING...
FAITHFUL...
ETERNAL.

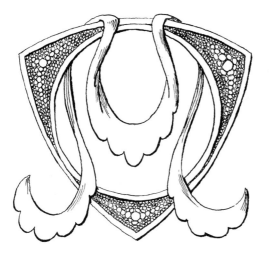

Beneath a Candle

My soul lies beneath this candle
a candle flickering its tiny light
for a few moments of serenity
this naked hand must in essence . . . write
of this soul

My soul lies beneath this candle
imprisoned, craving to be free
but as the moment of the hand endures
it contemplates, eternity.

My soul lies beneath this candle
the light becoming very dim
a last fleeting second it yearns
this soul to be released of him.

My soul lies beneath this candle
the existence of light is gone
naked and still and silent it lies
my soul awaits the lamenting dawn.
my freedom found.

The magnitude love achieves is
measured by its
          strength of giving,
          perception of understanding,
          faith of purpose
     through the passage of time.

A CHILD'S DREAM

How soft his face as he looked upon
The knight, with strength undaunted
Resting on the blood soaked earth
His mind of wars, was haunted.

Let this child erase your tears
of these things they know not of
For in the eyes of a little child
there is sincerely love.

He watches clouds as they amble by
and feels the breeze caressing
but does he see, into this face
affection, that's Gods blessing!

Then for a moment their eyes did meet
and the tears within his eyes
disappeared, as the night was born
For there he slowly died.

This little child of natural beauty
can only give in innocence, unspoiled
for man who sets the wars a-churning
uproots this little child he toiled.

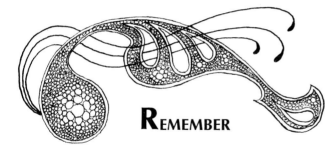

REMEMBER

when you ran along the rocky caves
discovered the ocean's white capped waves
when you dreamed of crystal clear lagoons
making love, in youth, by the light of
        the moon
when you saw the sun in all its splendor
touched a rose so soft and tender
felt the rain against your cheek
saw a fawn so shy and meek
when you played in the snow of yesterday
or slept in the barn on a mound of hay
when you planted your garden in early
        spring
or sat by a campfire while everyone sings
remember the swimming hole where we
        used to go
or the flower bed you used to hoe
remember the touch of a hand or the smile
        on a face
or the home that was blessed by your
        parents' grace
the little green tree so happy and bright
that was dressed all in colors on that
        christmas night
or the sounds of the birds or the stars in
        the sky
or your home-made kite you used to fly
remember, remember these things that
        you've done
    and think of your youth when you're
        teaching your son.

Children feel their hearts a-burning
Let them live their natural yearning

It is truth which makes man great . . .
for in truth lies all the virtues of
the human soul.

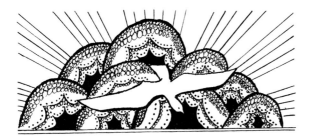

Follow your heart

I know the sun will rise every morning, even when there is fog. I know the whippoorwill sings melodious songs because I have heard them from the enclosure of my room. I know the sky is blue looking through the haze, that the grass is green even when I stand in the desert. I know the branches of trees dance to the movements of the wind even though now it is still. I know flowers have beautiful smells, that the ocean never sleeps and that snow falls upon high mountains. I know deeply, that all human beings are beautiful if they are born free to follow their hearts.

It has been said, long before these written words, that if you build an archway for your heart, with neither lock nor door, life will pass freely in harmony with your senses.

TOUCH ... your friends, your lover; a stranger, then they are a stranger no more. Hold them, feel the beauty of their skin, their face, their hair ... as you would touch the delicate petals of a carnation or put your hand in a gentle stream or feel the sand beneath your feet or climb upon the rocks and crags of the shoreline.

LISTEN . . . to their words, their breathing, their heartbeat, their footsteps on the carpet of leaves as they come to you . . . as you would listen to the rain or the deer running through the forest or the bark of a dog or the cascading of a waterfall or a tiny breeze.

SEE . . . . . . the expressions on their face of their different moods. See in their eyes the longing for love, companionship and a meaningful purpose to their lives. See their body move uniting themselves with life. See their hands create their being . . . as you would see a tidepool, the splash of a wave, a new portrait made by falling snow, the landscape of a valley, the changing of a sunset.

SPEAK . . . . to them of love, of the harmony of nature, of quiet understanding among men, of the simple things in life in which one can find peace, of the truth you have found . . . as you would speak to God.

Ride the crest of the wave to the shore.

Follow the river till it merges with the ocean.

Look at the clouds till they disappear.

Watch the sun rise, its path across the sky, then vanish.

When you have experienced these things you will know your heart . . . follow it.

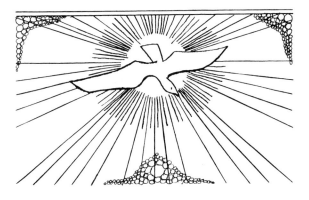

When you have freed yourself from the dogma and conditioning of your society, where will you go? To those things you love.

Let your mind and your actions explode with awareness as you light your forgotten lanterns of happiness, as you find a peaceful clearing in the jungle of your society.

Love is everywhere. It is the night sky where the stars smile. It is the field of wheat dancing in the wind. It is the waves sculpturing the rocks. It is in the sound of music, in man's creation of art. It is a seed nourished by two human beings.

Love will find you.
You will find love, if . . .
LOVE BECOMES
YOUR ATTITUDE

WALTER RINDER

Walt is the personification of the troubadour within us all. He lives out our fantasies through his travels, his experiences, and those he meets along the way. We share the feelings through his writing.

"Hi, you look a little down—like to talk about it?" You turn and there's Walt, his warm smile demolishing the wall of loneliness. He's been alone and dejected in many different environments. He's seen the drop-outs, the street people, the flower children, the runaways, and he is as one with them.

Walt is the "successful" poet who never allowed his achievements to become part of his living. The restlessness that was born in Chicago, a Gemini, grew up in Southern California and dropped out of college to wander the country. He is "home" in a house he built along a river in a forest not far from Portland, Oregon.

He has channeled just enough energy in specific directions to become an accomplished poet, photographer, and artist. The balance of his boundless energy is carefully invested in life. Those who read this book will enjoy reading Walt's personal philosophy in *Love Is My Reason* and sharing his unique gifts in his numerous other books of poetry and prose.

OTHER BOOKS BY WALTER RINDER

In AURA OF LOVE, Walter Rinder uses gentle, sensitive words and photographs to celebrate the little-understood value of self-image in love. 64 pages, soft cover, $3.50

FOLLOW YOUR HEART by Walter Rinder is a simple yet haunting description of the fullness, the tenderness that any man or woman will need to follow his heart. 64 pages, soft cover, $2.95

In THE HUMANNESS OF YOU, Walter Rinder combines an exciting, sensual and philosophical exploration of nature, its abundance and wisdom; a celebration of people -- family, friends, strangers; and a search for love and happiness, giving and receiving. 128 pages, soft cover, $4.95

SPECTRUM OF LOVE by Walter Rinder is a sensitive prose-poem that expresses all of the power, honesty, and commitment of love. 64 pages, soft cover, $2.95

THIS TIME CALLED LIFE by Walter Rinder is "such a completely beautiful book...here is writing of the highest quality illustrated by a remarkable photographs of nature and people." -- *Los Angeles Times*. 160 pages, soft cover, $4.95
(Also available in cloth edition, $7.95)

In WILL YOU SHARE WITH ME? Walter Rinder shares his love and desires, fulfilled and unfulfilled. Sensitively illustrated with his own photographs. 128 pages, soft cover, $4.95

LOVE IS MY REASON by Walter Rinder is a positive approach to life and love in which Walt speaks of our vast human potential. 128 pages, soft cover, $4.95

In WHERE WILL I BE TOMORROW? Walter Rinder "speaks...in prose, poetry, and eloquent photography of the love of a man for another man." -- *The Lambda Book Club*. 144 pages, soft cover, $4.95

Available at your local book or department store or directly from the publisher. To order by mail, send check or money order to:

CELESTIAL ARTS
231 Adrian Road, Suite MPB
Millbrae, CA 94030

Please include 50 cents for postage and handling.
California residents add 6% tax.